DISCARDED

My Mother's Keys
by Jeanette Hinds
Jane Eva Ellen, Photographer

My Mother's Keys
© 2002 Jeanette Hinds
Photos © 2002 Jane Eva Ellen
Published by
Lone Oak Press
1412 Bush Street
Red Wing, Minnesota 55066
info@loneoak.org
ISBN 1-883477-43-3
Library of Congress Control Number: 2001099088
No reproduction of any part of this work
is permitted without the written
permission of the author or artist except for
samples used in connection with a review.

Thanks to John Calvin Rezmerski, writer-in-residence
at Gustavus Adolphus College, St. Peter, Mn. for
the foreword, and to Diane Glancy, professor of English
at Macalester College, St. Paul, Mn. for the kind words.

Contents

FOREWORD

I. IF ONE NO LONGER HAS THE LAND BUT HAS THE MEMORY OF LAND, THEN ONE CAN MAKE A MAP

Waiting	7
Cellar Doors	9
Red Lantern	11
Cow Barn	13
Simplicity	15
Sheltered	17
Rituals of Fire	19
Rituals of Water	21
Connecting Trees	23
Fulfillment	25
Lesson in Vigilance	27
Meditation on a Plow	29

II. IN A DARK TIME THE EYE BEGINS TO SEE

Sympathy Cards	33
Canopies	35
Postscript	37
The Lands She Gave Me	39
Two Plates for Widows	41
Hair Pieces	43
Triptych in Ivory	45
Last Walk	47
The Last Unlocking	49
Keys to the '63 Rambler	51
My Mother's Country Road	53
Yellow Key	55
Of Leaves and Locks	57
Her Tallest Place	59
What Angels Leave	61
Skeleton Key	63
Author	65
Editor and Photographer	65

Foreword

Read this book in the morning so you can think about it all day. Jeanette Hinds goes leaping over nostalgia to the miracle inside memory. "We knew our duty toward cows," she tells us. She captures not just present-time feelings about the past, but more importantly, the feeling of the old days, and she brings that past feeling up into present clarity.

I have seldom read anything as moving as her latter-day grief at the smallness of her mother's world, a "four-walled island" in which Hinds can now gratefully understand her mother's generous nudges toward knowledge of a far wider world. This is a book about learning, learning from books and from the lives of family and neighbors, learning that the world is full of contrasts and that neither member of a contrasting pair is superior to the other.

This is also a book about preserving the names, the personalities, the activities of a family and its environs. Any family is lucky to have a preserver who thinks, feels, speaks, and sings like Jeanette Hinds. Her daughter Jane's photographs, clear and matter-of-fact, provide important and vivid contrast that supplies context for the lyricism of the poems.

                        John Calvin Rezmerski

I.
IF ONE NO LONGER HAS THE LAND BUT HAS THE
MEMORY OF LAND,
THEN ONE CAN MAKE A MAP
Anne Michaels

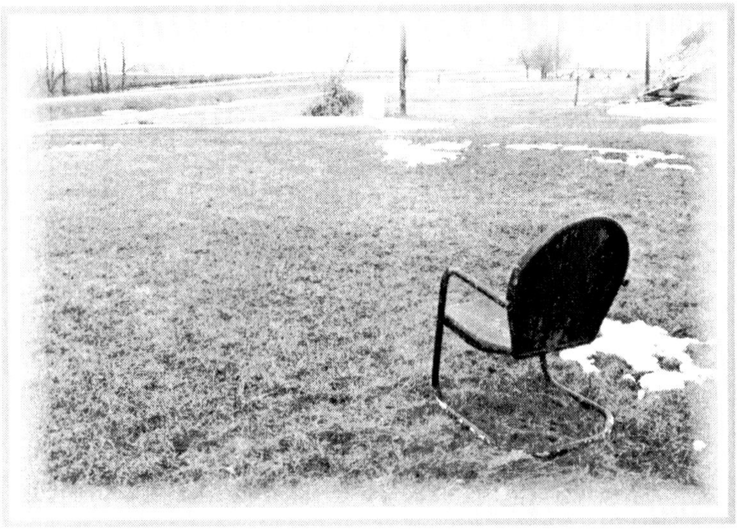

WAITING

Her gabled farmhouse stands solidly
among the seasons:
    April rain
    summer lightning
    September willows at sunset.

A sturdy Norwegian mother,
she sat in a metal chair
to meditate - hour after hour -
    on life
and the root-laden land.

Now, her empty metal chair
faces flat horizons
along last patches of snow.

From sleep of land; sleep of death
   she, like her beloved turf,
     awaits the first
       green
     awakening.

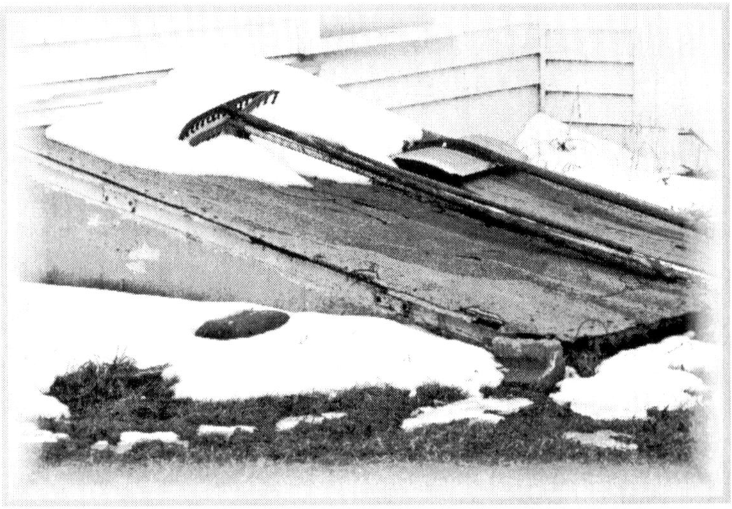

Cellar Doors

I could pull back massive wood
to uncover the alien winter,
but see where the last thaw
    exposes an abandoned rake
laid across tar papered doors
    like a rusty promise.

Angled against the house
    they meet in the middle,
    closed like a set of jaws.

Dank quarts of tomatoes
    dull under dusty days,
clustered paint cans stained
    with gray drips
    of dry relationships,
hard curls of centipede
    hung in spider webs
inhabit cold cellar depths...

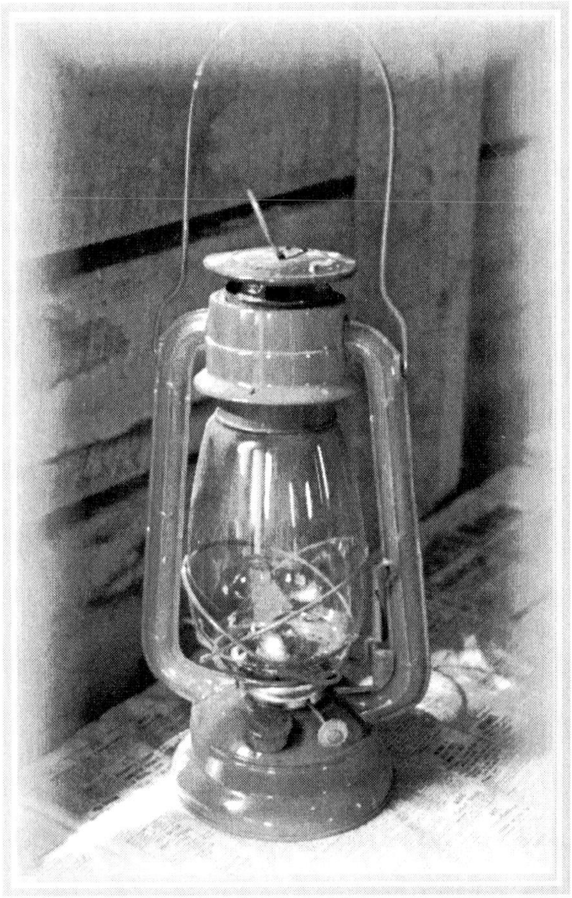

Red Lantern

Small lever lifts glass globe.
Pungent with kerosene, a wick
held like a tongue between lips
    awaits match-fire.

Flame flares, then tames
with globe settled into place.

Carried, the lantern bobs jigtime
as my father's legs stride
across the yard to the barn.

Hung on a high nail,
its cone of light widens
across rumps of Guernseys
eager to empty milk-hard bags.

Along gutter edges
    I wait like a yellow kitten
        by memory's battered pan.

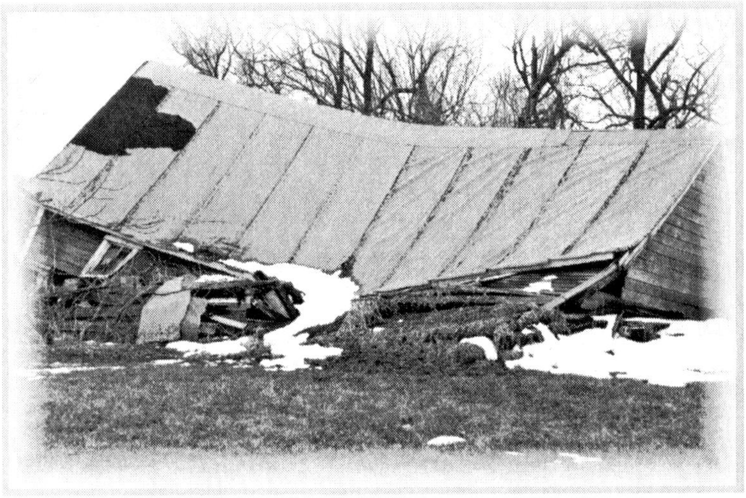

Cow Barn

the second tar paper roof
unrolled over leaking shingles
finally blew off piece by piece

it took a decade to fall

weathered siding, wrenched
loose under the gravity
of many snows, lay twisted

nails stuck out at all angles

the slant of rotted window pane
broke its own squares of glass
and looked out with empty eye

seeing final collapse ahead

we crept into the musty interior
to haul out stored bicycle parts
old wrenches, a bucket or two

no need for further shriving

draped in cobwebs, a heavy spike
angled into the wall, waited
for the lantern it held at milking

we stood listening, and almost heard

the rattle of stanchions when cows
stretch for a last bite of hay;
the whirr of a hand-crank machine

still separating years into
    skim milk
        &
      cream

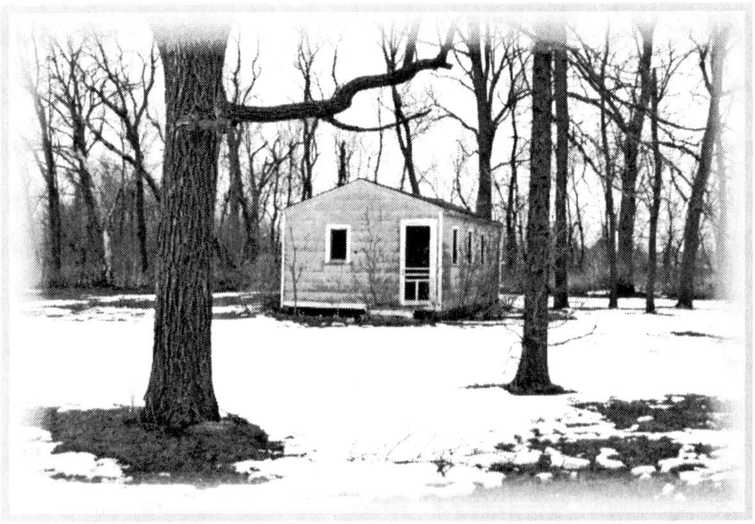

Simplicity

From one giant cottonwood
among pasture bogs,
we dreamed a cabin:

hauled home-sawed logs
    in a borrowed truck,
raised skeleton rafters
    smelling of raw wood,
pounded siding nails (our backs
    sweaty in sunshine),
scrounged discarded windows
    from the nuns' old music hall,
begged subflooring
    from the neighbor's scrap pile.

Two teachers with six children,
we raised an object lesson
and hoped it would cling
    closer than skin
    deeper than bone.

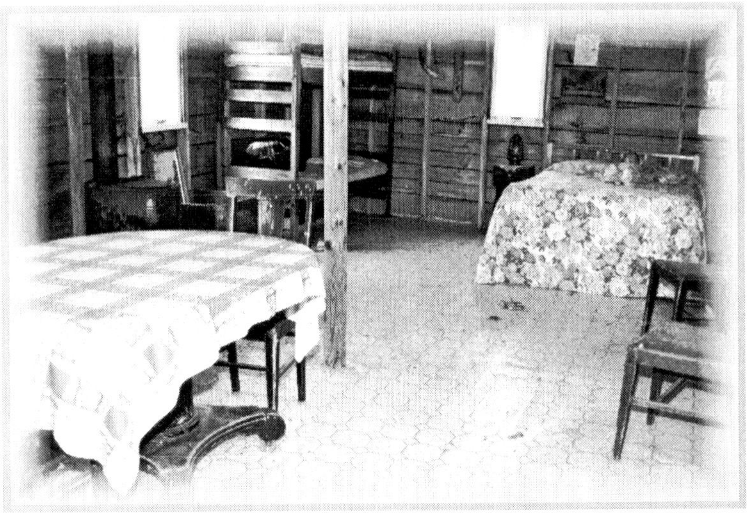

Sheltered

We furnished our cabin with
bunk beds salvaged from WWII,
army quilts, iron skillets,
unmatched plates and bowls,
an oak table from Uncle Carl…

We dined on
strawberries from the garden,
fried potatoes and pork-and-beans
served on red and white oilcloth
while the sun hung in the west—
a scarlet ball sliding behind
the dark edge of the cow lane.

In the pool of light
from a kerosene lamp,
we listened to
wind-music beyond small windows;
rain-music on the roof.

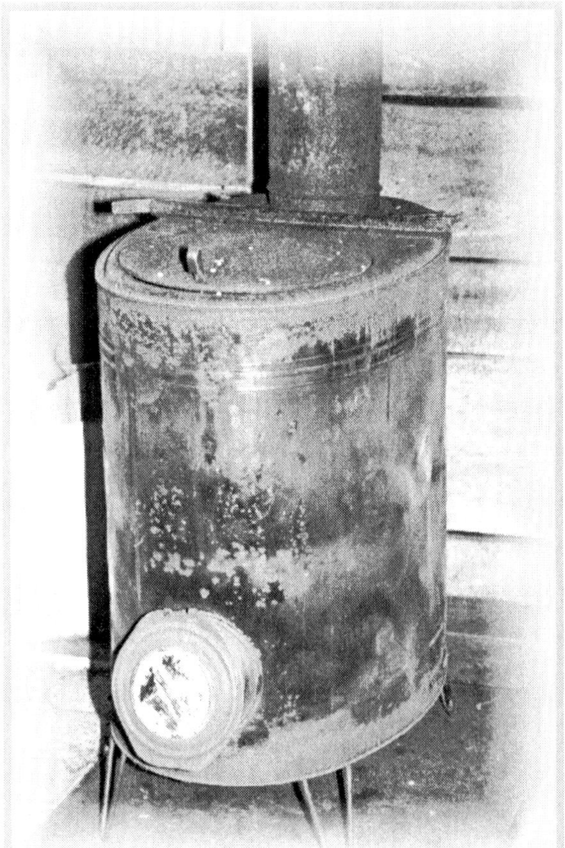

Rituals of Fire

We budgeted with care for the stove
    ordered from Sears
        unpacked from a cardboard box.

In frost-fringed Octobers, my husband
created the first sounds of morning:
    scrape of large lid pulled aside,
    crumple of newspaper,
    snap of kindling twigs,
    clunk of boxelder stove-lengths,
    chimney draft flipped up,
    bottom draft twirled open.
Full-fired like a central sun,
the metal sides glowed red.

Long after the stove rusted,
remembered fires remain.
A core of warmth sustains us
    as we walk across
the cold linoleums of the world.

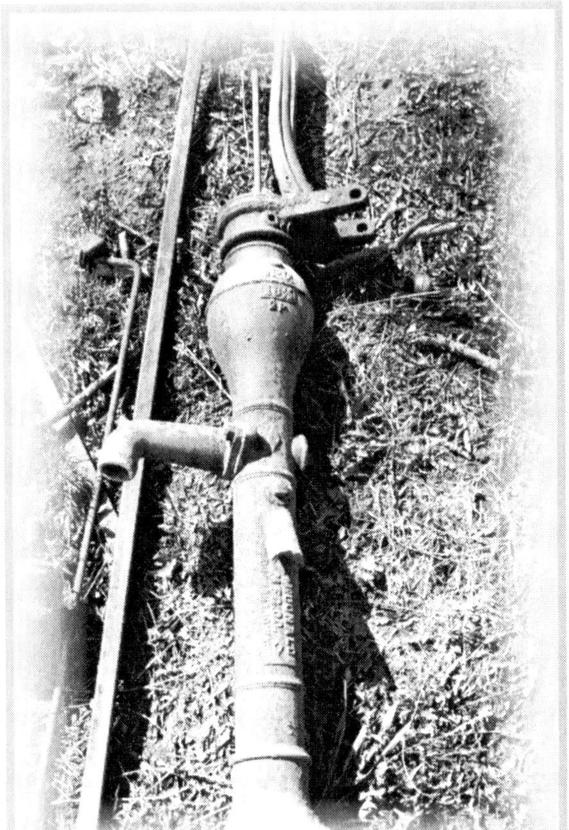

Rituals of Water

In the farmyard, the metal pump stood
bolted to thick boards of weathered oak.
Under the platform, heavy pipes
descended through layers of limestone;
connected with dark pools of cold water.
    We drank it from a tin cup
    hung on a wire by the well.

Or we carried a sloshing pail to our cabin
and set it on two wooden orange crates
alongside an enamel wash-dish.
    Dipper and towel hung
    on separate nails;
    soap softened in a bowl.

We knew our duty toward cows.
A long steel pipe led to the livestock tank.
Gripping the metal handle, we pumped
and counted—five hundred strokes.
Six Guernsey cows nudged
    each other aside—
wide noses dripping.

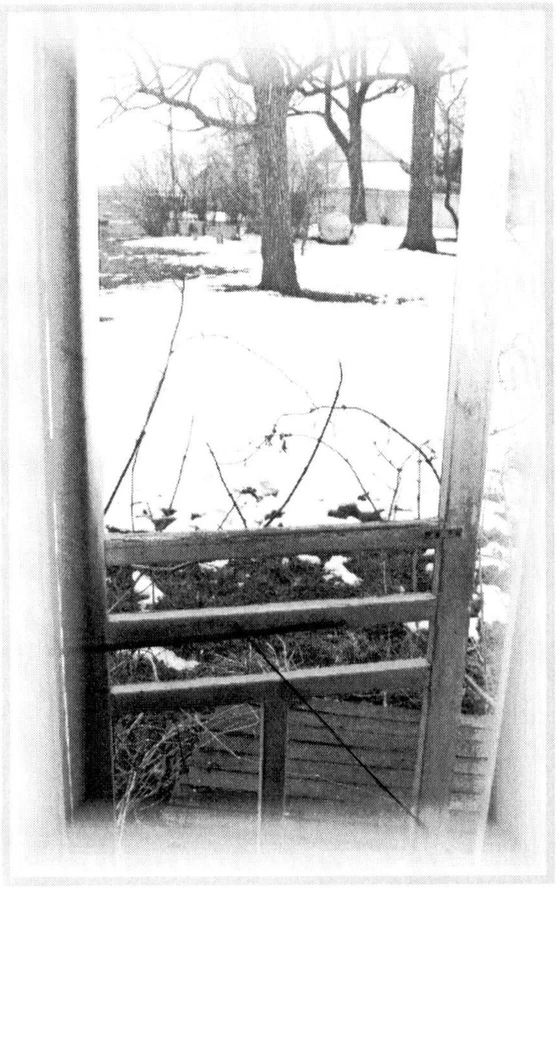

Connecting Trees

Black walnut trees connected common lawn
with the main farmhouse.
Lacy leaves and deep-grooved trunks
stood through daily sun or rain.
Every fall, they bore hard fruit.

Green staining husks
removed through a corn-sheller
revealed the damp nuts.
With discolored fingers, we spread
them to dry on tarps in the sun.

Our children learned
no nut breaks easily.
Only hammer, pick, and a thumb
bruised against the cracking stone
results in a shattered chamber.

Finally, among scattered shells, it lies –
a core of walnut, richly flavored.

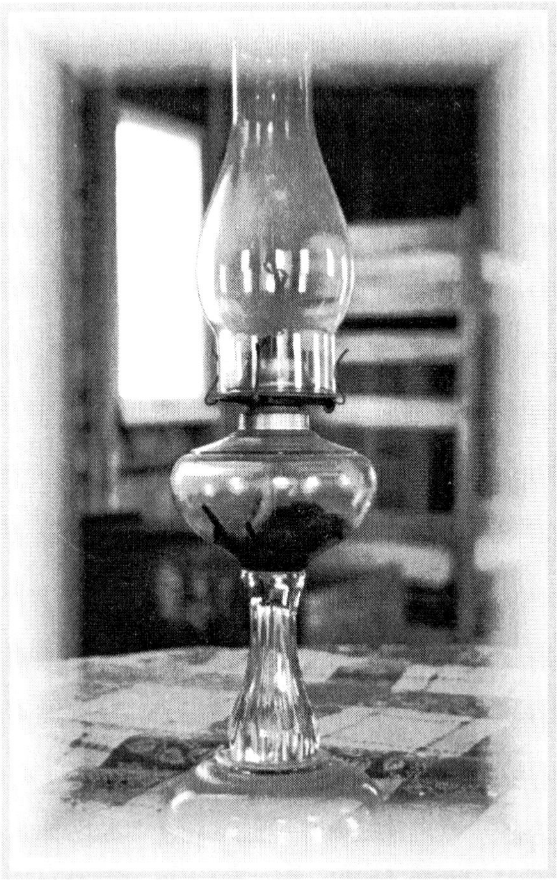

Fulfillment

My father milked cows at dawn,
plowed quack grass with a noisy Fordson,
checked brooder-house temperatures
after midnight lest baby chicks
crowd to their death under a cold hover.

But his eyes softened as he watched
grandchildren play tag in their pajamas
shouting under sunsets of summer trees
until lamplight through cabin windows
invited them to beds of renewing sleep.

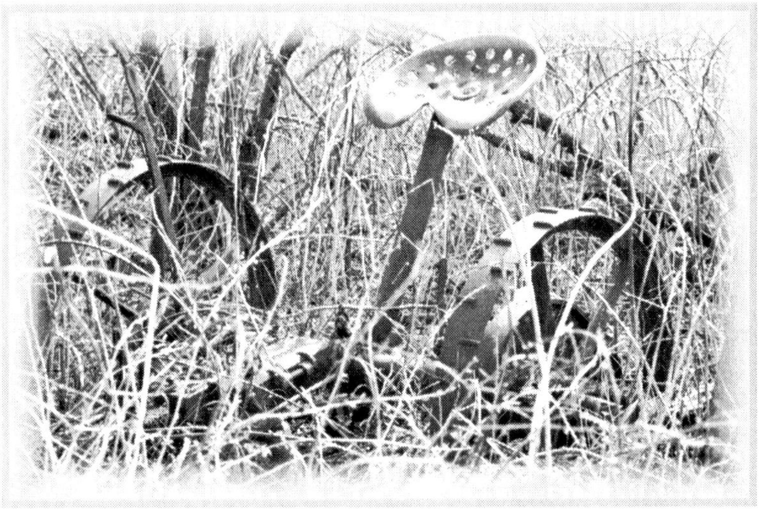

Lesson in Vigilance

Tangled stems of scrub boxelder
stand among the farm's rusted machinery—
sulky plow, quack-drag, cultivator,
    seeder with rotting box.

Buttock shape soldered
to a length of spring steel
forms the mower seat where her grandson sat
    when he mowed the cowpen.

Squeezing the lever, he lowered
the sickle bar and watched the blades
slide and whirr like noisy teeth
    cutting swath after swath.

Knowing the irrevocable slash
does not discriminate grass from legs
of a dog or a nest of cottontails,
he learned to ride through life
one hand steady on the lever.

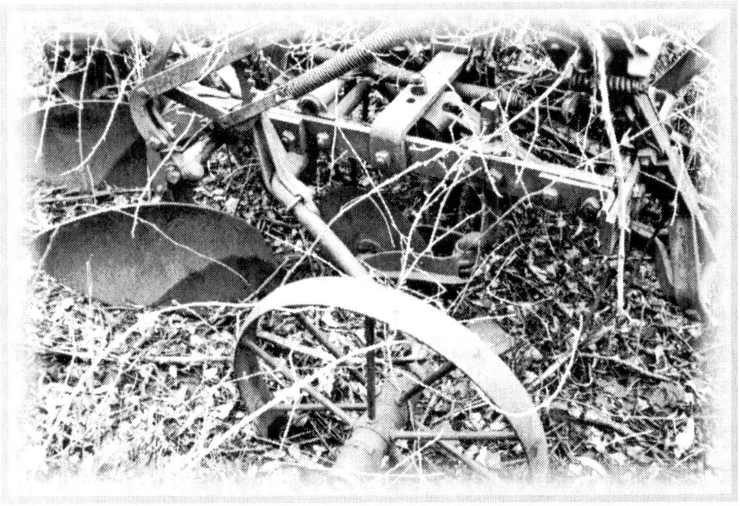

Meditation on a Plow

Rotted hitching-tongue, rusted plowshares,
spokes and hubs of unturned wheels
weather under brittle weeds. Once
     the plow broke loam into furrows;
     turned earth ready for planting.

Soon each hill of corn stood separate
like green yarn tying a black quilt.
Stretching through four-cornered wind,
morning mist, July sun, each stalk
     tasseled by late summer,
     swelled with ears of corn.

In September, green silk dried to brown,
kernels dented, dry stalks rustled at touch.
Slow-driving a wagon through the rows,
we broke ears loose with pegs on our wrists,
stripped the husks, tossed the yellow corn
into the wagon—fitted with a "bang-board"
so we couldn't over-throw.

Now I too am a plow:
     turning soil upside-down,
     making earth ready for planting,
     earning the rust when my day comes
     to lie near a slatted corncrib
     where each year the yellow
     of another crop shows through.

II.
IN A DARK TIME THE EYE BEGINS TO SEE
Theodore Roethke

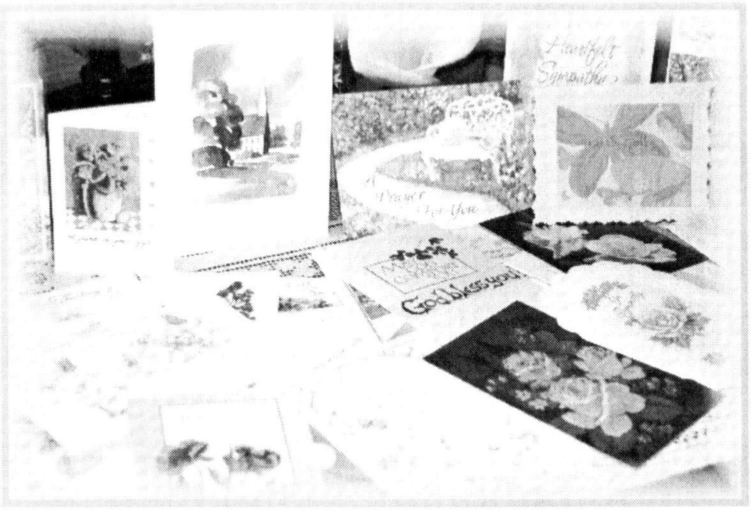
Heartfelt Sympathy
A Prayer For You
God bless you

Sympathy Cards

Sixty-two cards
grouped on the round oak table—
blue butterflies, white lilies
    "deep"; "heartfelt"

A note from Lila—
    red roses, extra large.
Maybe because she planned to visit
    and never found time.

From the Pastor,
    gold letters on white:
"Ever watchful...ever faithful
...everlasting is the Lord."

Like obituaries, the cards come once;
brief remark of a brick removed
    from family walls.

I stand close
    absorb the crash;
feel the cornerstone of home
    implode.

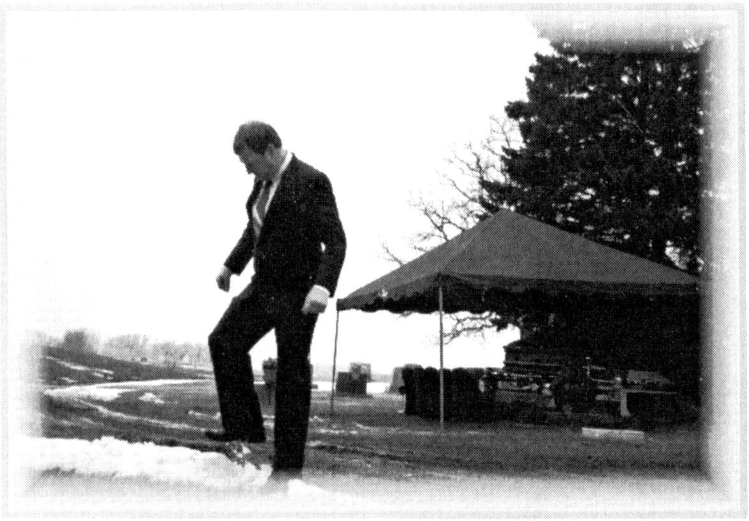

Canopies

On this coverlid day,
brown canvas stretches over poles;
shelters the cluster
of family and friends.
A shepherd-calm voice shields us
with promised mansions of Word;
with litanies of ritual prayer.

Under a sheaf of carnations,
the poised coffin
centered with strap and rope
will be lowered into
a concrete vault
and secluded by layers of earth
as soon as we leave.

My mother's body lies
shrouded in her best black blouse
under a curve of bronze lid—
pod within pod but the seed
slipped from the husk.

Back at the church, good ladies
set out sandwiches and cake;
prepare for the refuge of small talk.

Unsheltered, her grandson steps away
through February mud and left-over snow.
Keen-edged ice and naked cold moves in.
We, blood from her blood,
body from her body, sharply know
a canopy since birth
has been folded and stored away.

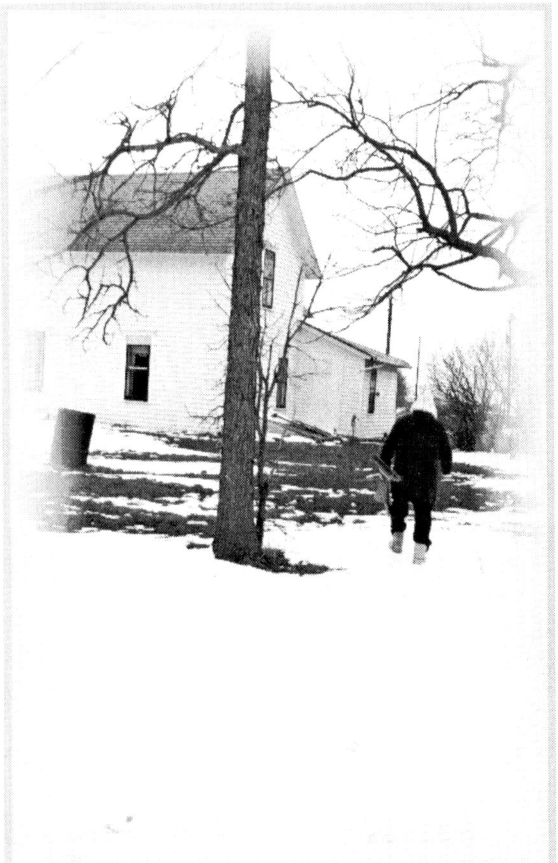

Postscript

Not knowing it was her last night,
I turned to leave and she said,
"I won't see you for a long time."

Now, in my own narrow room,
I answer, "Not true.
Morning is one sleep away."

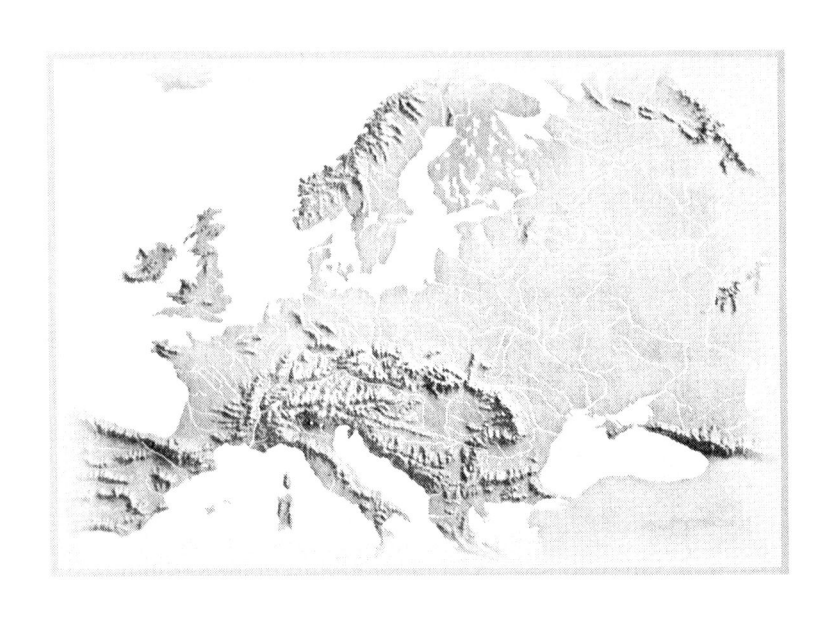

THE LANDS SHE GAVE ME

I open the yellow pages
  –Frye's Grammar School Geography–
closed for nearly a century.
Mildew odors rise from brittle paper,
Table of Contents shreds loose.

As a child studying relief maps,
my mother saw fjords of Norway leap
    over northern Europe
    like a lumpy dog
    with a smooth underbelly
    marked "Sweden".
Teddy bear Ireland floated
    with one Londonderry eye.

School seemed barely necessary
    for phonetic grocery lists;
    occasional notes.
Her sense of loss came
    hard and late…

When I skipped a grade,
we drilled multiplication tables
    – hour after hour –
in a game of steps
across the kitchen linoleum.
She gripped each flashcard
between forefinger and thumb.

As my inner map expanded,
small silences we both denied
lapped along our daily shores;
widened into a gulf
    beyond our ferrying.

    I still mourn when I think
    of her on a four-walled island
while I, reading under a kerosene lamp,
lived in the prairies of Rølvaag,
    the London of Dickens,
    the Russia of Dostoyevsky.

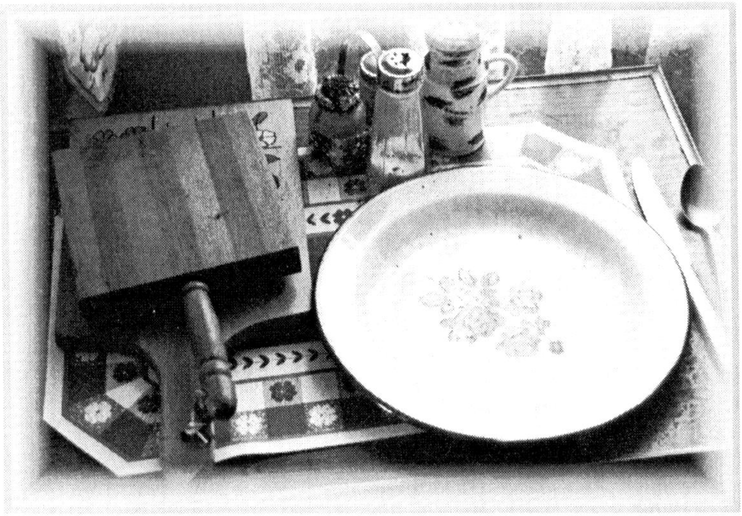

Two Plates for Widows

Plastic mat on a tray table
pulled up to the window—
Radio turned on
to break three dimensional silence—
Over and over, the widow's routine plate:
    hers, white enamel;
        years later
    mine, chipped pottery.

    Daily cadence of crockery
    circles and centers my hour.
    Today the shaker is empty,
    the salt has lost its savor.
    A microwave potato is
     like God—the same yesterday
    and today and forever.

My mother fried roundsteak
to the consistency of leather;
but she, who knew life is tough,
kept the discipline of shined plate—
clean, ready, centered with roses.

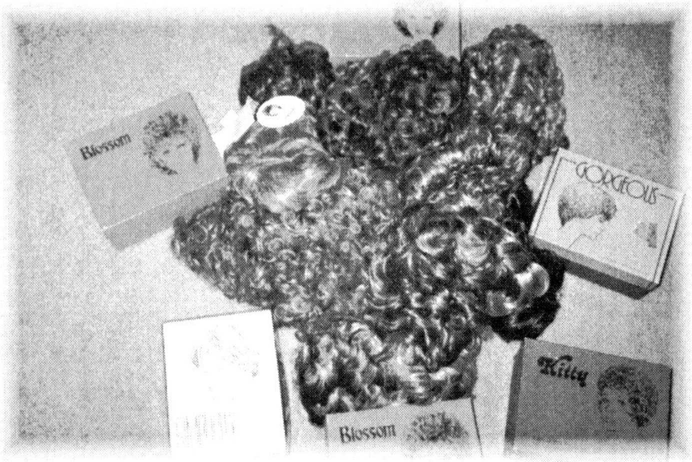
Blossom
GORGEOUS
Kitty
Blossom

Hair Pieces

In Flapper times, she cultivated bangs
    straight sides with frontal flip
    and close-tapered neckline
styled at the barber shop across the street.

In Young Motherhood, she wore a fluff
    clamped into curls
    by heating an iron
hung down a kerosene lamp chimney.

Depression times brought straitened days—
    brown bobby pins held
    smooth sides into place;
anchored a bun at the neck.

When Old Age locks of wispy hair
    let scalp shine through,
    she, defying silken loss,
bought fourteen K-Mart wigs.

She who never heard of villanelles
    taught our family females
    to wear a woman's rage
against the dying light.

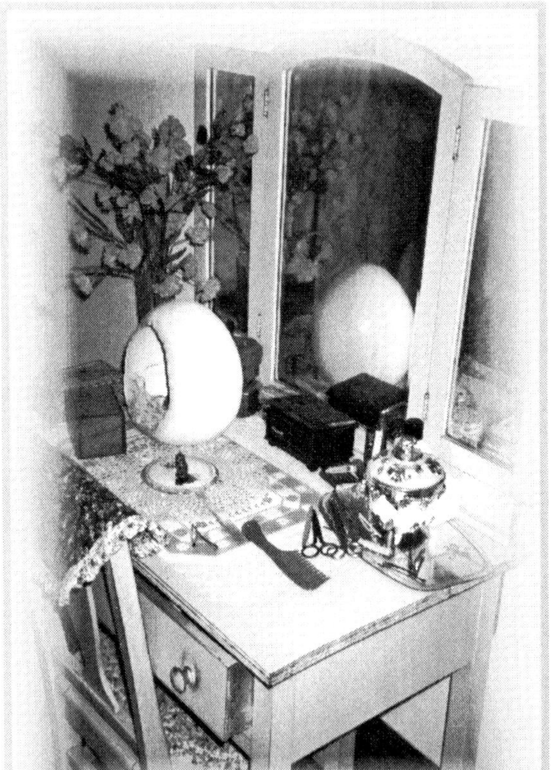

Triptych in Ivory

My mother's ivory dressing table
existed before I was born:
gloss-paint top
pull-out drawer
central mirror
flanked with side panels—
altarpiece for Narcissus.

Ritual reflected the years:
candle-bright lipsticks,
colognes like incense,
trays of Woolworth earrings,
a chalice of plastic roses,
and always, the small hand-mirror
 – final genuflection.

Now the ivory dressing table sits
in my granddaughter's bedroom.
How seldom she bends
toward mirrors of water.
Wise with Greek story,
she already understands
     a drowning god
       in love with his face
         dwindles to a common flower.

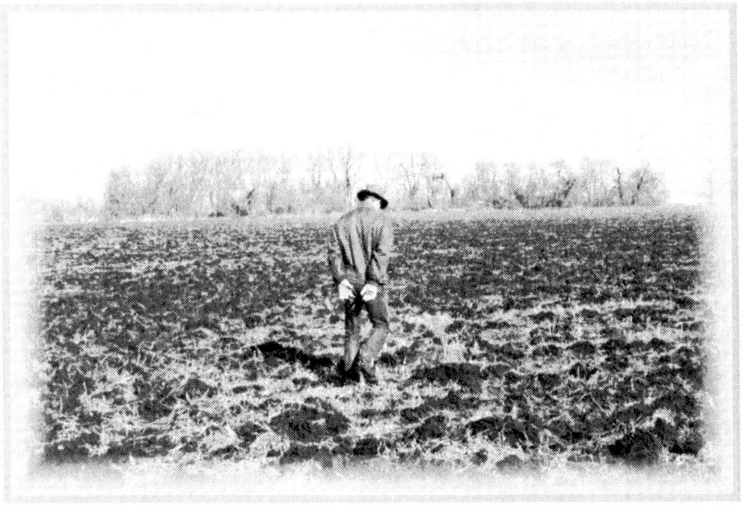

Last Walk

Her grandson, who turned fifty
in the spring she died,
    walks the land.
Already the new owner's blade
turns black furrows edged with last
season's stubbled corn.

A horizon of bare willows suspends
the greens of a coming year
in the long slow flow through woody
    fibers and cells.
Indifferent trees eventually
    will shelter a new crop of robins;
a cool twilight owl
    asking "Who?"
will not care who owns the land.

At mid-life, her grandson
    directs and measures each step
as he understands, like a weight,
how the latent and eternal land
    lies lightly pressed
under his heavy ephemeral boot.

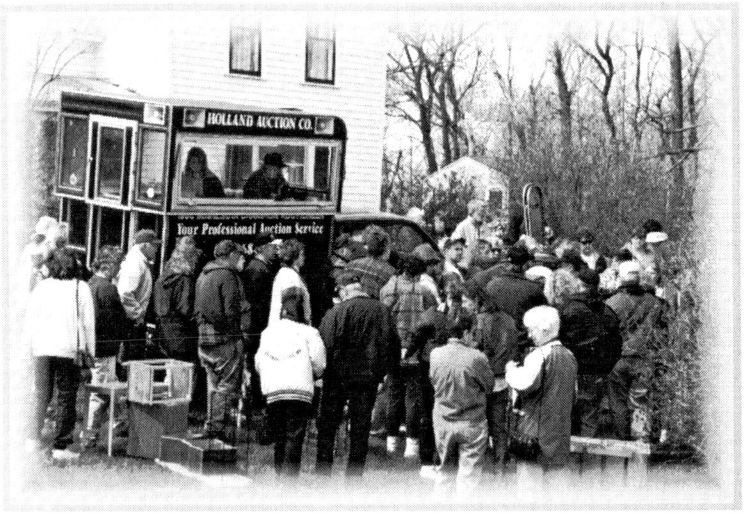
HOLLAND AUCTION CO.
Your Professional Auction Service

The Last Unlocking

Mother never threw a key away;
her top kitchen drawer jangled
    where they slid about.
Often she stood before a building in the sun
leafing through key after key after key.

To simplify life, I finally
ringed the tops with colored plastic:
green for shed housing the Snapper and Gilson,
red for granary holding Mission Oak chairs,
pink for garage and the Rambler
    that no longer ran,
purple for basement full of paint cans and jars,
yellow for the back door to the house.

Every evening, moving building to building,
she double-checked each lock.

She could never have imagined the auction:
strangers loading her bed into a pickup, or
carrying off pictures, ladders, cream cans—
and as the sun began to set,
all doors standing open,
    empty
        like startled mouths.

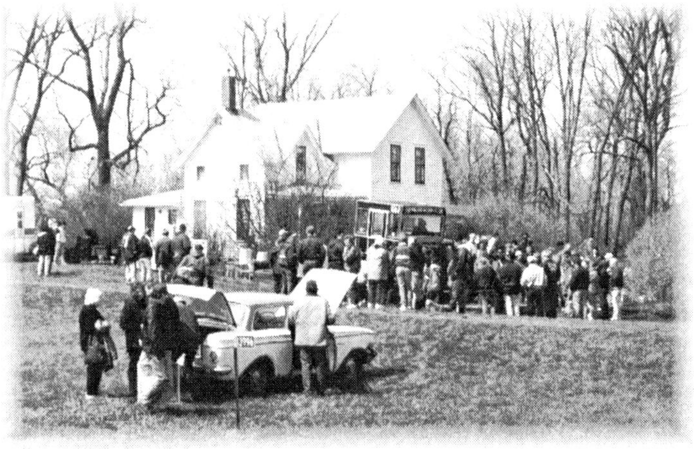

Keys to the '63 Rambler

Hood stands open, trunk lid lifted
like an old horse with jaws flung wide.
Farmers hope to discover whether age
has made the car "long in the tooth."
    It has.

Under the sun's white-hard truth
rusted fenders, cracked windshield,
shredded upholstery, flat tires
reveal and question a reason
    to be.

After housewares, the auction crowd
shifts and encircles. "Forty, forty.
Now fifty. Who'll make it sixty...
Sixty, sixty..." The mallet falls.
    "Sold for $60!"

I hand over title card and keys
to a stranger who cannot know:
three-mile trips to Ellendale Creamery,
grocery stops at Lerberg's store,
Sunday drives along Beaver Lake.
    These I keep.

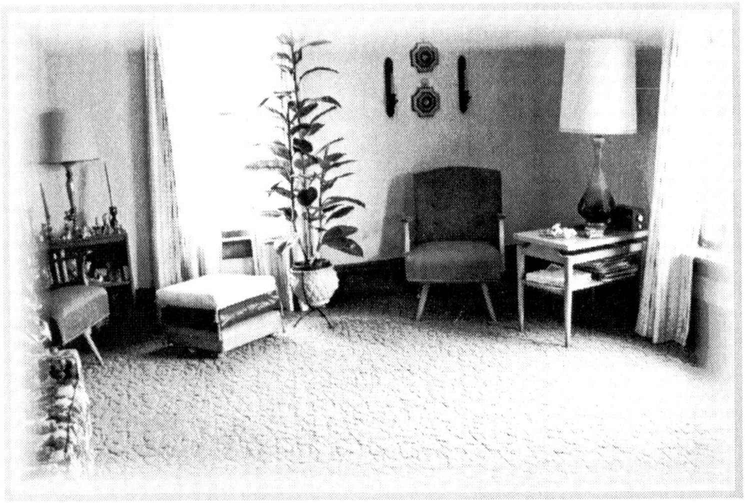

My Mother's Country Road

Once, thinking she needed a larger vision,
we took my mother to Nova Scotia:
    Parliament Hill in Montreal,
      La Place Royale restored in Quebec,
        Bluenose Ferry crossing Bay of Fundy.
At Peggy's Cove with lighthouse
    on slabbed rocks along the Atlantic,
        she'd had enough.
"*When* will we be back in the United States?"

Motel rooms made her homesick
for gold carpet under evening lamplight,
knicknacks arranged on a bookcase,
curtains drawn back from windows
overlooking a yard slanting toward lilacs.

She could not read Canadian French directions:
    "sud, nord, est, ouest"
All her life, she knew how to spell "home."

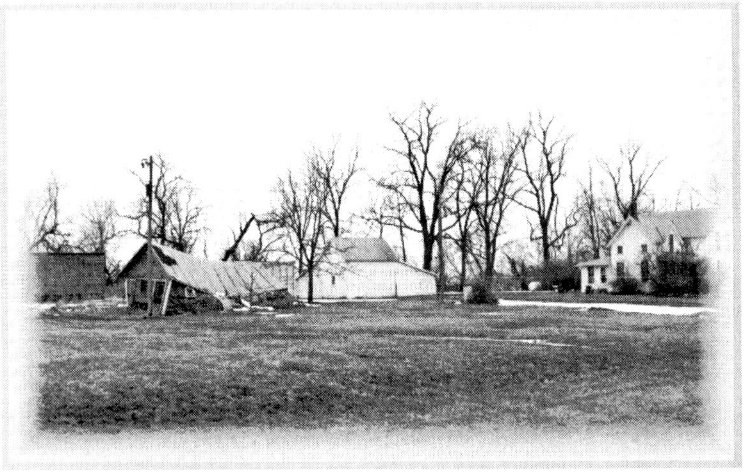

Yellow Key

At age 94, my mother,
enraged at the necessity,
moved to Town Hall Estates.
Only her body lived there.

Almost weekly, we drove 60 miles
    to check and re-check her farm.
Our conversation took on the routine
    sameness of the road.

As we curved past Jensen's farm
    her white farmhouse
    broke into view
a gabled and protective hen
sitting on an expanse of green.

"Where are the keys?
    You've got the keys."
"No, Mom, they're in your purse.
    The one with the yellow ring."

As we pulled in the driveway,
she scrambled out. I watched her—
    key in hand
    bending to open
    the center of the world.

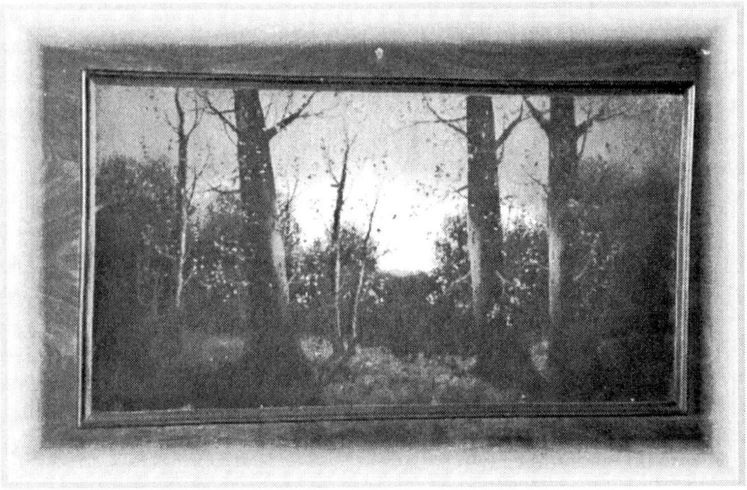

OF LEAVES AND LOCKS

Irrevocable door
    locked.
Me on earth side,
plump, warm, grainy.
Ethereal *mother*
no longer inhabiting wig
black slacks
earrings of yellow glass.

Every time we left the farm
she asked,
"Are you sure the door is locked?"
She'd check the deadbolt,
rattle the doorknob...

Mission Oak davenport and chairs,
lamps bought with Gold Bond stamps,
kitchen curtains of Woolworth lace...
Only this wooden door kept home
safe from the vandal-world
while she lived out her days
in the Board-and-Care.

The first picture she owned
still hung on the dining room wall.
Sunset glinted on scattered leaves;
a few clung to dark trees.
    Often, like a mantra, she'd say,
    "It's hand-painted, you know."

Now her last leaf has fallen.
The picture hangs in *my* dining room.
Across from a western window,
    it catches sunset light.

Yesterday I installed a deadbolt
    on my front door.

Leaves keep falling.

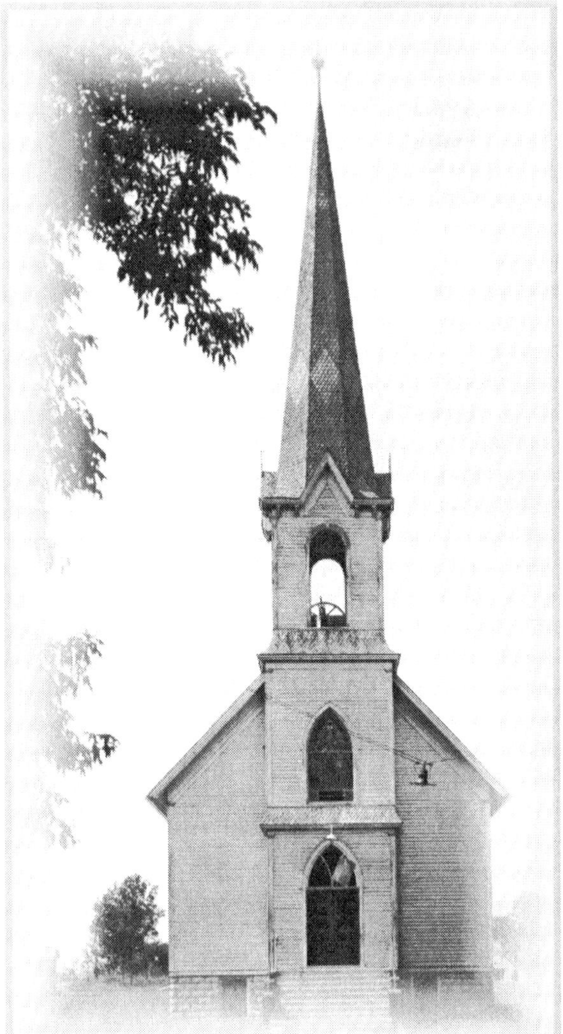

HER TALLEST PLACE

As near to heaven as they could climb,
Norwegian settlers from Søgn and Telemark
built a spire and belfry tall against the sunset's fire.
Clapboard white, the church crowned the village hill.

Stained glass images glowed within:
        three drops of water from a shell
        the rite of grape and bread
        descending flight of Spirit Dove
        the wooden cross of martyrdom.
Where oak pews shone in rows of honeyed light,
her family spent a time on small but holy ground.

In God's own high-arched house, an inner sight
revealed the small Imperfect Self. Yet she
who had not heard of Julian's mystic showings knew:

"Sin is necessary, but all shall be well.
All shall be well; and all manner of thing shall be well."

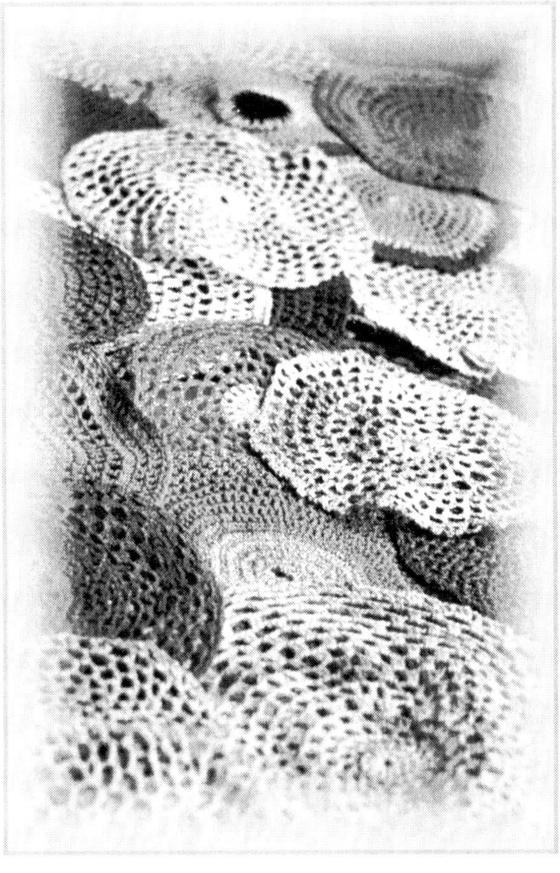

What Angels Leave

Monet's *Grainstacks*
    painted under varieties of light;
        Grant Wood's Iowa farmland
        female contoured;
    Grandma Moses' sleighs and steeples
        in primitive primaries...

    unaware of gene pools
  she carried them; we all carry them

    back; back
to some Cro-Magnons equipped with saliva and clay
    crawling through dark caves
    to create rhinos or bursts of bison
        depicted with extra legs
        to denote speed.

    unaware of gene pools
  she carried them; we all carry them

I remember her hooked needle crocheting
    from a dense center—
      looped stitches
    interlocked row on row
variegated threads: circled pastels
    bold red, blue, and yellow,
        or
    beige oblongs glinting gold,
        or
    rectangles carefully bound.

beyond routines of work and food and sleep,
beyond a muddy February funeral day—

      her small doily
      held in my hand
        solid-color
      green as lifetimes of grass,
          endures.

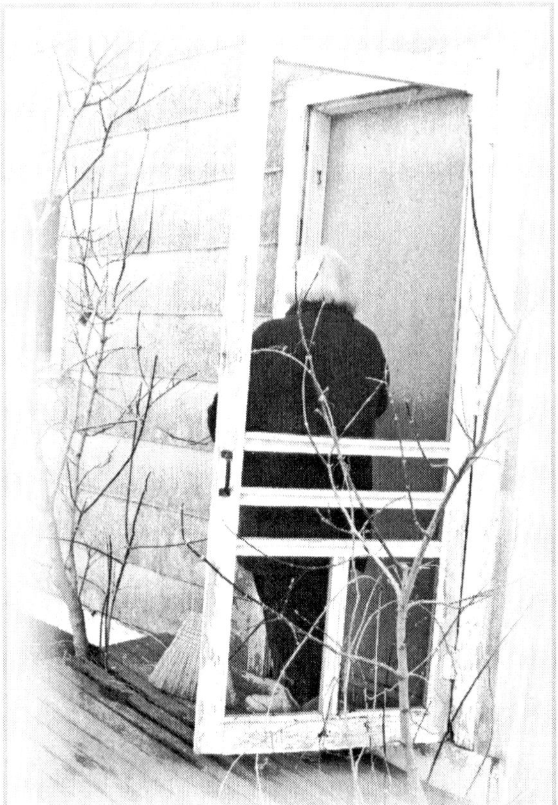

Skeleton Key

sturdy, long of shank,
a skeleton key
opens old doors with rectangular plates
and round-headed key holes

lacking a carefully notched
precision
its weight of heavy metal
lay cold in my hand

fumbling through self-doubt, I stood
jangling my key in the lock
listening
for the small creative click
that opens truth

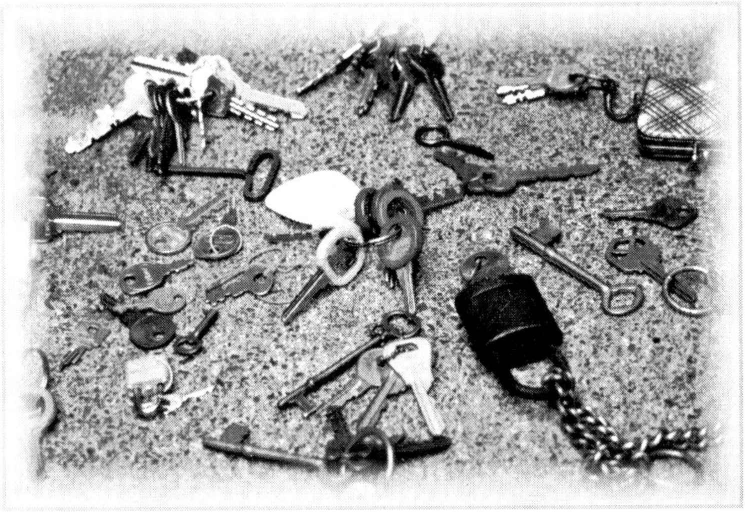

Author

Jeanette (Mangskau) Hinds was born in Ellendale, Minnesota where her father clerked in Lerberg's General Store for 30 years. When she was in seventh grade, the family purchased a small farm three miles from the village. Her mother continued to live on the farm until she was 94 years old.

As an only child, Jeanette was never lonely because she began writing on the farm. Her first poem was published when she was 13. She continued to write and publish while raising six children. Her husband taught science. She holds a B.S. degree from Minnesota State University, Mankato and an M.A. degree from the University of Wisconsin at Madison. This is her second poetry chapbook.

Editor and Photographer

Jane Eva Ellen is the author's youngest child. While growing up, the family made weekly visits to her grandparent's farm. After her grandmother's death, she took photographs of the farm to preserve her family's history.

Jane, an editor and writer, holds a B.A. degree from Gustavus Adolphus College, and an M.F.A. degree from Hamline University. She lives with her husband and young daughter in Minneapolis.